HALSEY'S DECISION:
ORGANIZATIONAL FAILURE
AT LEYTE GULF

TURKEY TROTS TO WATER GG FROM CINCPAC ACTION COM
THIRD FLEET INFO COMINCH CTF SEVENTY-SEVEN X WHERE
IS RPT WHERE IS TASK FORCE THIRTY FOUR RR THE
WORLD WONDERS

DAVID L. BROOKS

NIMBLE BOOKS LLC

Nimble Books LLC
1521 Martha Avenue
Ann Arbor, MI, USA 48103
http://www.NimbleBooks.com
wfz@nimblebooks.com
+1.734-330-2593
Copyright 2014 Nimble Books LLC

Printed in the United States of America
ISBN-13: 978-1-60888-1-628

Contents

Introduction

As dawn lightened the sky at 0627 on 25 October 1944, Rear Admiral Clifton "Ziggy" Sprague surveyed his command, Task Unit 77.4.3 (TU 77.4.3), known by his call sign, Taffy 3. The six escort carriers, mere 20-knot Kaiser-built merchant-ship hulls with a flight deck on top, were arranged in a circle, within an outer circle of three destroyers and four destroyer escorts, steering a southwesterly course about 40 miles off the coast of Samar Island.

Admiral Thomas Kinkaid's Seventh Fleet invaded Leyte island on 20 October, placing Lieutenant General Walter Krueger's Sixth Army ashore. Yesterday, 24 October, Admiral William F. Halsey, covering the landings, moved his main striking force, the fast carriers of Task Force 38 (TF 38), into position and began day-long attacks on what the Americans called the Japanese Center Force, in the Sibuyan Sea, as they moved toward San Bernardino Strait where they could enter the Philippine Sea north of Taffy 3. The Center Force, commanded by Vice Admiral Takeo Kurita, with five powerful battleships (including *Yamato* and *Musashi*, the two largest ever built), 10 heavy cruisers, two light cruisers and 15 destroyers,[1] was beat up so badly in

---

[1]This and the following Japanese force tallies are from H.P. Willmott, *The Battle of Leyte Gulf: The Last Fleet Action* (Bloomington, IN: Indiana University Press, 2005), 88.

the course of the day that they turned back from the Strait in mid-afternoon.

That evening, Halsey's fliers had discovered another Japanese force, Vice Admiral Jisaburō Ozawa's Northern Force, with four carriers, two converted battleships (their aft turrets were removed and a short flight deck installed), three light cruisers and eight destroyers. Halsey left Task Force 34 (TF 34), commanded by Vice Admiral Willis Lee with four battleships, five cruisers, and fourteen destroyers, to guard the strait against the Center Force as he took his carriers north to deal with Ozawa.

And then, last night and into the wee hours of the morning, Rear Admiral Oldendorf's Seventh Fleet gunfire support group of six old battleships, four heavy cruisers, four light cruisers, and twenty-eight destroyers, had virtually annihilated Vice Admiral Shōji Nishimura's van of the Japanese Southern Force, consisting of two old battleships, one heavy cruiser, and four destroyers, in the Surigao Strait as they tried to force entrance into Leyte Gulf and attack the American transports. Oldendorf was even then chasing the follow-on force of Vice Admiral Kiyohide Shima's three cruisers and four destroyers back up the strait.

The Japanese had been routed and all Ziggy Sprague had to do was sit aboard his flagship, the escort carrier Fanshaw Bay, monitor Taffy 3's air activities and, when necessary, direct their movements.[2] A Combat Air Patrol (CAP) for the ships in Leyte Gulf took off at 0530, and by 0607 Taffy 3 also had four torpedo planes and two fighters for Gulf anti-submarine patrol (A/S), as well as its own CAP and A/S patrols in the air.[3]

By now morning battle-stations have been secured, and as Admiral Sprague watches light north-easterly winds push rain squalls across a gently rolling sea,[4] the crew are going below for breakfast or some shut-eye, and the ship settles into her morning routine.

At 0643 Sprague receives a radio message from the A/S to the north of Taffy 3: "Enemy surface force of four battleships, four heavy cruisers, two light cruisers, and ten to twelve destroyers sighted twenty miles northwest of your task group and closing in on you at thirty knots."[5]

The admiral is not impressed. Obviously this young aviator had spotted the battleships of Admiral Lee's TF 34 and had broken radio silence, potentially giving away the position of Taffy 3,

---

[2]James D. Hornfischer, *The Last Stand of the Tin Can Sailors* (New York: Bantam Books, 2004), 132.

[3]Samuel Eliot Morison, *History of United States Naval Operations in World War II*, vol. 12, *Leyte, June 1944–January 1945* (1958: repr. Edison, N.J: Castle Books, 2001), 246.

[4]Morison, *Leyte*, 250.

[5]Hornfischer, *Last Stand*, 136.

to report this stupendous news. Sprague yells "Tell him to check identification" at air plot.[6]

Then things begin to happen too fast. At 0645 lookouts sight anti-aircraft fire to the north. Are our ships firing at our planes? At 0646 Fanshaw Bay makes an "unidentified surface contact" on her radar and her radio watch reports "Japs gabbing" on the fighter-interception net.[7] And then at 0647 the A/S patrol radios: "I can see pagoda masts, and I see the biggest red meatball flag I ever saw on the biggest battleship I ever saw."[8]

Ziggy Sprague knows his ships are in trouble. His 20-knot carriers and his paltry 5-inch guns firing a 54-pound shell with a range of about nine nautical miles, which can not penetrate battleship or cruiser armor, are no match for even the smallest of the Japanese battleships, which could do 30 knots and fired three-quarter-ton 14-inch shells twenty miles.[9]

How could this have happened? Where was TF 34? Where was Halsey?

At 0657 Sprague ordered a course change to due east, to open the range and turn into the wind to launch planes. A minute later, the Japanese battleships opened up at a range of 15 nautical miles. Where was Halsey?

---

[6]Morison, *Leyte*, 246.
[7]Morison, *Leyte*, 246; Hornfischer, *Last Stand,* 136.
[8]Hornfischer, *Last Stand,* 137.
[9]Ibid.

Sprague sends an urgent contact report in plain language at 1701, giving his position and that of the Japanese and asking for all available assistance.[10] Where the hell was Halsey?

To understand how it happened that Taffy 3 was left to face Kurita's battleships and cruisers, we need to look at the organizational context in which Halsey and others made decisions. Then we'll need to have a brief look at the battle, paying attention to the exact sequence of events. Next, it will be necessary to look at certain events in more detail, to understand just how certain decisions were arrived at. And lastly, we'll consider the judgments of some of Halsey's professional contemporaries and of later historians before we're in a position to render a balanced judgment of our own.

The Context of the Decision

No commander makes a decision in a vacuum. He not only makes his decisions with regard to the tactical situation as he understands it, but also in the context of a set of institutions which define what he can do, who he is responsible to, and what task he must accomplish. The important institutions for trying to understand how it happened that Ziggy Sprague was left to face the might of the Center Force by himself are the command structure of the Leyte operation, communications between the

---

[10]Morison, *Leyte*, 250.

fleet commanders, the orders Halsey operated under, and the staff he worked with.

Command structure

The United States never achieved the unity of command in the Pacific Theater that was achieved in the European Theater. Before the war, inter-service rivalries prevented either the Army or the Navy from subordinating themselves to the other and so separate commands were established sharing an area of responsibility. This was the case at Pearl Harbor immediately before the war, where Admiral Husband E. Kimmel and Lieutenant General Walter C. Short divided the duties of the defense of Pearl Harbor. Even the obvious failure of this "command-by-mutual-cooperation"[11] could not overcome inter-service rivalry to place the Pacific Theater under a unified command.

To avoid sharing areas of responsibility the Joint Chiefs of Staff (JCS) divided the Pacific Theater between two geographical commands: in 1942 General Douglas MacArthur was appointed Supreme Commander of the Southwest Pacific Area (COMSOWESPAC), while Admiral Chester Nimitz was the Commander in Chief of the Pacific Fleet (CINCPAC) and the Pacific Ocean Areas (CINCPOA).

---

[11]*Investigation of the Pearl Harbor Attack*, 79th Congress, 2d Session. S. Doc. 244, Vol. 3, 150. http://www.ibiblio.org/pha/pha/congress/part_0.html.

This worked well enough while operations were confined to a particular area of responsibility under a commander responsible for that area. And to keep it that way, area boundaries were sometimes moved, as happened in the Solomons campaign when the boundary between the two area commands was moved one degree west, so that Nimitz's ships wouldn't sail in MacArthur's waters.[12] But the plan of campaign settled on in September 1944 called for MacArthur's Southwest Pacific Forces to work their way up the coast of New Guinea, occupy Morotai and Salebaboe Island, and land on Mindanao, while Central Pacific forces under Nimitz take Peleliu, Yap and Ulithi in the Carolines. The two forces would then converge for an invasion of the central Philippines.[13]

And when they did? A unified command required either MacArthur subordinating himself to Nimitz, or Nimitz giving up control of the Pacific Fleet's fast carrier task forces to MacArthur. One has trouble envisioning Douglas MacArthur subordinating himself to anyone, even for so cherished a goal as the reoccupation of the Philippines, just as it is extremely difficult visualizing Nimitz relinquishing control of his carriers an army officer. And the JCS found it impossible to impose a unified command.

---

[12]Morison, *History of United States Naval Operations in World War II*, vol. 4, *Coral Sea, Midway and Submarine Actions May 1942–August 1942* (1949: repr. Edison, NJ: Castle Books, 2001), 261.

[13]Morison, *Leyte*, 11-12.

As usual where personalities and politics play a role, the actual outcome was muddle and fudge.

For the invasion of Leyte there were four commands which had no common commander short of the President of the United States.[14] Douglas MacArthur commanded Lieutenant General Walter Krueger's Sixth Army and Vice Admiral Thomas Kinkaid's Seventh Fleet, as well as some air forces. Chester Nimitz commanded the Pacific Fleet and the Third Fleet of Admiral William F. Halsey, as well as the VII Army Air Force. General H.H. Arnold commanded the XX Army Air Force and took direction from the JCS, and General J.W. Stilwell of the China-Burma-India command controlled the XIV Army Air Force.

While the air forces are irrelevant to our narrative, the naval commands are vital. Although both MacArthur and Nimitz reported to the JCS, the JCS, being a committee, did not speak with one voice. Any dispute between MacArthur and Nimitz would have had to have gone to the individual who commanded them both: the Commander in Chief of the armed forces of the United States, President Franklin D. Roosevelt.[15] Rather than force a turf fight which would have had to go to the President, the two commanders tacitly agreed to live with the status quo.

---

[14]Ibid., 55-56.

[15]Richard W. Bates, "The Battle for Leyte Gulf October 1944. Strategical and Tactical Analysis." Unpublished Research Document, U.S. Naval War College, Newport, R.I.: 1953. Vol. I, sec. (3), 15-18.

As Samuel Eliot Morison observed, "In view of the magnitude of the Leyte operation, the overall plan was fairly simple; but the command set-up was complicated."[16]

Although this command structure has often been blamed for the leaving Taffy 3 to face the battleships and cruisers of the Center Force,[17] we shall see that it was not the only element contributing to the situation.

Communications

Given this command structure, where Kinkaid of the Seventh Fleet and Halsey of the Third Fleet did not report to a common superior who was close by and who could coordinate their plans and actions, coordination and close communication between them was absolutely vital.[18]

The Navy of the period had two means of radio communication: a short-range, VHF voice radio called Talk Between Ships (TBS) and the long-range method of radio telegraphy using Morse code, either encoded or in plain language. The sensible solution for coordination between Kinkaid and Halsey would

---

[16]Morison, *Leyte*, 55.

[17]See, for instance: Kent S. Coleman, "Halsey at Leyte Gulf: Command Decisions and Disunity of Effort" (master's thesis, Fort Leavenworth, Kansas, 2006), 3 and 97; D.C. Robertson, "Operations Analysis: The Battle for Leyte Gulf" (Unpublished Research Document, U.S. Naval War College, Newport, R.I.: 1993).

[18]Robertson, "Operations Analysis," 10.

have been for the two fleet commanders to agree on a frequency which they would monitor for direct communication between the two flagships.

This, however, was not authorized by MacArthur.[19] MacArthur, ever mindful of his authority and unwilling to risk being undermined by two navy commanders chatting where he couldn't hear, ordered that all communications between the fleets be broadcast to the rear base at Manus, in the Admiralty Islands, 1500 miles away off the coast of New Guinea, for rebroadcast on the Fox Schedule, which was copied by every ship and command in the Pacific.[20] The radio operators at Manus were understandably swamped with traffic during the Leyte operation, as two U.S. fleets engaged in four major battles in two days. Radio traffic came pouring in and priority messages piled up. The harassed operators could only make a guess at which priority messages were most urgent, and not much else got through. But this cumbersome and time-consuming method—even urgent messages often took an hour and a half to reach their recipients-- ensured that every message passed between the fleet commanders came across MacArthur's desk.

---

[19]Evan Thomas, *Sea of Thunder: Four Commanders and the Last Great Naval Campaign 1941–1945* (NY: Simon & Schuster) 2007, 212.

[20]E.B. Potter, *Bull Halsey: A Biography* (Annapolis, MD: Naval Institute Press, 1985) 290; Thomas J. Cutler, *The Battle of Leyte Gulf: 23-26 October 1944* (Annapolis, MD: Naval Institute Press, 1994) 159; Coleman, "Halsey at Leyte Gulf," 48-9.

Orders

The orders from Nimitz that Halsey operated under required three things.[21] First, Halsey and the Third Fleet were required to "cover and support" Southwest Pacific Forces landing in the central Philippines. Second, Halsey and the Third Fleet were required to "destroy enemy naval and air forces in or threatening the Philippines Area." These were standard orders issued to forces covering landings in the Pacific. They required the covering force to give immediate assistance to the landing forces and to destroy such enemy forces as directly threatened the landing forces.

But Halsey and the Third Fleet were also given a third task: "In case of opportunity for destruction of major portion of the enemy fleet offers or can be created, such destruction becomes the primary task." Halsey's order to "destroy enemy naval and air forces in or threatening the Philippines Area," limited him to those enemy forces directly threatening the landing forces. The order for the "destruction of major portions of the enemy fleet" had no such limitation. Halsey was free to chase down the Japanese wherever he thought he could catch them, so long as such destruction contributed to the protection and support of the landings. And by making such destruction "the primary task,"

---

[21]For discussions of Halsey's orders, see Morison, *Leyte*, 58-60; Bates, "Battle for Leyte Gulf," I:15-18; Vego, Battle for Leyte, 126-128.

his orders for the destruction of the enemy fleet overrode his orders to cover and support the landings.

That particular sentence seems to have been inserted into the orders of the covering force commander after the invasion of Saipan and the subsequent Battle of the Philippine Sea. Admiral Raymond A. Spruance, as commander of the Fifth Fleet during the invasion of Saipan, was only given orders to "cover and support" the amphibious landings. When Japanese carrier forces attempted to intervene, Spruance offered battle and, in destroying more than 500 Japanese aircraft, almost ended Japanese carrier air power in the war. But he refused to leave the landings unprotected to chase down the Japanese carriers, fearing that a second Japanese force was at sea waiting to slip in behind him and break up the landings.[22] Although three Japanese carriers were sunk during the battle (two by U.S. submarines), six others got away and Spruance, although defended by both Admiral King, Chief of Naval Operations (CNO), and Nimitz, was severely criticized within naval aviation circles for not pursuing the carriers.

Halsey, an old friend of Spruance's, did not criticize Spruance himself,[23] but was well aware of what others were saying. And

---

[22]Morison, *History of United States Naval Operations in World War II,* vol. 8, *New Guinea and the Marianas March 1944–August 1944,* (1958: repr. Edison, NJ: Castle Books, 2001), 252.
[23]Potter, *Bull Halsey,* 272.

one can easily imagine Halsey vowing not to let the Japanese carriers get away again if he had a chance to destroy them.

This was not the first time Nimitz had included that task in his orders to his covering force commanders. He had employed that exact sentence, word for word,[24] in his Operation Plan for the invasion of Ulithi and Palau two months earlier. But in that case the operation was entirely under the control of Nimitz himself as CINCPAC. But in the circumstances of the Leyte operation, Nimitz had inadvertently created a situation in which the covering forces of CINCPAC's Third Fleet had an overriding responsibility to destroy the enemy fleet, even if it meant abandoning his task of supporting the landing forces under COMSOWESPAC.

And there was also something curiously missing from Halsey's orders. Although Nimitz, in his Operation Plan 8-44, directed that "Necessary measures for detailed coordination of operations between the Western Pacific Task Forces and the forces of the Southwest Pacific will be arranged by their respective commanders,"[25] nothing in his operations plan or in Halsey's operations order required that Halsey obtain MacArthur's or Kinkaid's concurrence for any of his operations, or even advise them as to his plans.[26] Cooperation between Kinkaid and Halsey

---

[24]Bates, "Operations Analysis," I:17.
[25]Ibid., I:15.
[26]Ibid., I:17.

was little more than a pious hope which found no expression in the orders actually issued.

Staff

A commander relies on his staff for many things, not the least of which is the exploration of the options he has in the situation he finds himself in. Staffs also tend to reflect the way the commander does business. A quiet, professional, business-like approach on the part of the commander will find an echo in the quiet, professional, business-like approach of his staff.

Halsey's staff was boisterous, creative, argumentative,[27] and tremendously admiring and loyal to the man known to his subordinates as "Admiral Bill."[28] He liked having his staff around him arguing out a problem, and he encouraged them to argue their position against anyone. The most junior officer on his staff was free to disagree and argue with his deputy, his chief of staff, or Halsey himself, if that officer thought they were wrong.[29]

But when Halsey thought the problem had been hashed out and the options sufficiently explored, he did not dither but promptly made a decision. He would point his finger and say

---

[27]Thomas, *Sea of Thunder*, 227.
[28]Potter, *Bull Halsey*, 2.
[29]Ibid. 245.

"Okay, lads. That's it. That's what we'll do."[30] Discussion was then at an end and his staff knew the Admiral expected them to carry out his decision.[31]

Halsey was decisive. He took tough decisions promptly and stuck by them, not allowing himself or his staff to re-open old debates. That was a strength in the difficulties and confusion of battle. But it was also a weakness.

The Battle in Brief

Most accounts of the battle follow individual Japanese and American forces as they maneuver and clash, taking up another force and battle when the account of one battle is complete. This makes for an attractive narrative but disguises the confusion that arises when all of these forces are operating simultaneously. As we are interested in what happened when, we will follow a fairly strict chronological account of the action.

23 October

The first Japanese force to be spotted was the Center Force, found at 0116[32] by two American submarines, *Darter* and *Dace*, in the Palawan Passage. They radioed a sighting report and attack, sinking two heavy cruisers and crippling a third. Halsey

---

[30]Thomas, *Sea of Thunder*, 158; Potter, *Bull Halsey*, 245.

[31]Potter, *Bull Halsey*, 245.

[32]Times follow Morison in *Leyte*, chaps. 9-14, unless otherwise noted.

received the sighting report at 0620. Neither Halsey nor Kinkaid
expected the Japanese fleet to challenge the Leyte landings,[33] but
with a Japanese battleship force out, others would be too. They
had to be found.

At about noon on the 23 October, TF 38 was 260 miles
northeast of Samar. During the night of 23/24 October, Halsey
moved his ships toward the Philippines. Rear Admiral Bogan's
Task Group 38.2 (TG 38.2) moved close to the San Bernardino
Strait; Rear Admiral Sherman's TG 38.3 took a position north of
Bogan to cover the west coast of Luzon; Rear Admiral Davidson's TG 38.4 moved south of Bogan near Leyte Gulf. The
three groups were now in position for aerial searches to fan out
and cover the entire archipelago. Vice Admiral McCain's TG
38.1 was on its way to Ulithi for rest and replenishment.

24 October

TF 38 launched early morning searches, and at 0812 a plane
from Bogan's Group 2 sighted the Center Force. But the Americans were not the only ones flying that morning. At 0820 search
planes from Ozawa's Northern Force sighted Sherman's Group
3, the northern-most group. Ozawa steamed south to close the
distance.

Halsey received the sighting report of the Center Force at
0822, and at 0827, bypassing the TF 38 commander, Vice Admi-

---

[33]Thomas, *Sea of Thunder*, 171.

ral Marc Mitscher, he ordered Sherman and Davidson to concentrate on Bogan's group off San Bernardino Strait and launch air attacks on the Center Force, and he recalled McCain's group from its replenishment mission.

But the Japanese got in first licks. At 0833 three raids of 50 to 60 land-based planes attacked Sherman's Group 3, north of the Strait. All but one were shot down or turned back. That one, a lone Yokosuka D4Y "Judy" dive bomber, planted a bomb at 0938 on the flight deck of the light carrier *Princeton,* starting fires that would force the abandonment and sinking of that ship by U.S. forces at about 1750.

Other players showed up to the table at 0905, when planes from Davidson's Group 4 in the south spotted Nishimura's van group of the Southern Force in the Sulu Sea. They attacked with little result, but the American now knew there were at least two Japanese surface forces at sea, and they suspected the carriers must be at sea as well. The Southern Force was spared further attack as Davidson moved north to close on Bogan's Group and launch strikes on the Center Force.

Bogan's Group 2 launches a strike at 0910 which hit the Center Force at 1026. During the day TF 38 launched five strikes totaling 259 sorties. They sank the super battleship *Musashi,* crippled a heavy cruiser, and caused minor damage to other ships.

The Japanese were not idle. At 1145 another scout plane from the not-yet-discovered Northern Force spotted Group 3. Ozawa launched a 76-plane strike on Sherman's Group and then began to steer a box, playing bait, trying to lure Halsey away from the American landing forces in Leyte Gulf. The strike accomplished nothing and the planes landed at Japanese bases on Luzon.

A Vth Army Air Force bomber at 1155 reported Shima's group of the Southern Force near the Cagayan Islands. Admiral Kinkaid, the Seventh Fleet commander, who was with the landing force in Leyte Gulf, figured out what the Japanese are up to and at 1215 alerted his command to prepare for a night surface engagement against the Japanese Southern Force trying to force Surigao Strait.

After the Center Force endured wave after wave of air attacks, American planes report at 1400 that it had reversed course and was steering westerly, as if to retire. Actually, they were at first milling about trying to avoid air attacks, but actually did set a course of 290° and retired at 1500. Meanwhile, at 1430 Ozawa detached Rear Admiral Matsuda with the two converted battleships and light forces from his Northern Force and sent them south to attack the Americans. And at 1443 Kinkaid ordered Rear Admiral Oldendorf to form up the old battleships, cruisers, and destroyers of the gunfire support group across the northern entrance to Surigao Strait.

At 1512 Halsey sent a message headed "Battle Plan" to all Third Fleet task force and group commanders, and to Admirals King and Nimitz, saying four battleships and supporting warships "will be formed" as TF 34 "to engage decisively at long ranges" under the command of Vice Admiral Lee. Although not an information addressee, because it's just a plan and does not affect his operations, Admiral Kinkaid saw the message and read it as an order to form TF 34 (as does King and Nimitz).

As the afternoon wears on, the missing Japanese force was finally found. At 1540 two pilots from Davidson's Group 4 sighted Matsuda's force built around the two converted battleships, and at 1640 the main body of Ozawa's Northern Force, the four carriers, was sighted. Now that all the Japanese forces were accounted for, Halsey laid his plans.

At approximately 1700, Kinkaid launched a search to his north by PBY-5 Catalina "Black Cats," which didn't find anything.[34]

Halsey, at 1710, sent a clarification to his previous "battle plan" message by TBS to two of his Task Groups: "If the enemy sorties TF 34 will be formed when directed by me." Because this direction was given via short-range radio, neither Kinkaid nor King nor Nimitz received it.

---

[34]Morison, *Leyte*, 289-90.

Kurita, unnoticed by the Americans, reversed course at 1714 and made another try for the San Bernardino Strait. At 1935 the Center Force was spotted by a night-flying reconnaissance plane from Independence in Bogan's Group 2, on course 120°, headed for the Strait.

While that message made its way to the flagship, Halsey, having digested the flash reports concerning damage to the Center Force and believing that it "had been badly mauled with all of its battleships and most of its heavy cruisers tremendously reduced in fighting power and life,"[35] ordered his staff shortly before 2000 to have TF 38 concentrate to go after Ozawa's Northern Force carriers. He then retired to bed.[36]

Shortly after Halsey retires, the report that Kurita's Center Force has turned back toward San Bernardino Strait was received in flag plot.[37] But orders to the Task Groups were already being written. At 2022, orders went out for Bogan's Group 2 and Davidson's Group 4 to steam north at 25 knots to join Sherman's Group 3 for an attack on Ozawa, while McCain's Group 1 was ordered to complete refueling and join up. Rear Admiral Robert "Mick" Carney, Halsey's chief of staff, puts the following message on the Fox Schedule for Kinkaid, King, and Nimitz: "Enemy force Sibuyan sea 1925 position 12 45N 122 40E course 120

---

[35]Ibid. 194n30. See also, Willmott, *Battle of Leyte Gulf,* 113.
[36]Thomas, *Sea of Thunder,* 385-6; Potter, *Bull Halsey,* 296.
[37]Thomas, *Sea of Thunder,* 385.

speed 12 knots. Strike reports indicate enemy heavily damaged. Am proceeding north with three groups to attack enemy carrier force at dawn."[38] Kinkaid assumed that the three carrier groups are headed north, but that the battle line, TF 34, was formed and left behind to guard the strait.[39]

Another night reconnaissance plane, at 2030, picked up Kurita's Center Force about 25 miles closer to the Strait than previously reported. And at 2120 the Center Force was sighted off Aguja Point of Burias Island by a night flier, making 20 knots about 50 miles from the entrance to the Strait. Meanwhile, at 2110 Ozawa recalled Matsuda's battleships and turned his carriers to a southwesterly course to close the American task force.

And things began to heat up down South as well. At 2236 PT boats spotted the van of the Southern Group on radar, and at 2250 they made a visual sighting of it. Two minutes later they were spotted by the Southern Force. The Japanese maneuvered and illuminated, and the fight with the PTs was on, lasting until 0213. The lead group of PTs had it radios knocked out, so one boat headed up the strait to contact the second section to get the sighting report out.

At 2320 the night fliers lost track of the Center Force and were pulled off to search for Ozawa's Northern Force. By 2345

---

[38]Carl Solberg, *Decision and Dissent: With Halsey at Leyte Gulf* (Annapolis, MD: Naval Institute Press, 1995), 119.

[39]Potter, *Bull Halsey*, 296.

TF 38 Groups 2, 3, and 4 had rendezvoused and Halsey returned tactical command of TF 38 to Mitscher.

25 October

The PTs reported the presence of the Southern Force at 0010. The report was received by Rear Admiral Jesse Oldendorf, commander of Seventh Fleet gunfire support, at 0026. He already had his six old battleships, eight cruisers, and numerous destroyers arrayed in depth blocking passage from Surigao Strait into Leyte Gulf.

At the far end of Samar Island, Kurita's Center Force passed through San Bernardino Strait and entered the Philippine Sea at 0035. Shortly after, at 0100, *Independence* launched night searches to the north to try and find the Northern Force carriers.

At 0155 Admiral Kinkaid ordered Rear Admiral Thomas Sprague, commanding TG 77.4 (the 16 Taffy escort carriers) to launch three daybreak searches, one of them to cover the sector north of the carriers in the direction of San Bernardino Strait.

Meanwhile, TF 38's searchers found Ozawa's Northern Force carriers at 0205 and a second plane reported them at 0235. The position report contained an error, however, leading Mitscher to believe Ozawa was 120 miles nearer him than the 210 miles that actually separated the two forces. Five minutes later, Mitscher, believing the Japanese are within 100 miles, thought it prudent to place a battleship screen between the carriers and the Japanese.[40] TF 34 was formed, with all six fast battleships, seven cruisers and 17 destroyers, Vice Admiral Lee commanding.

The action in the Surigao Strait heated up at 0300 as destroyers begin to attack the van of the Southern Force with torpedoes. They crippled a battleship (which later sank), damaged the other battleship, sank two destroyers and damaged a third. The American cruisers opened fire at 0351 and the battleships followed at 0353. Only a damaged Japanese cruiser and a destroyer survived the onslaught. Admiral Shima's second section of the Southern Force, about 40 miles behind Nishimura, was attacked by PT boats at about 0315, and a light cruiser was damaged. By 0425 Shima, having streamed past the burning and sinking remnants of Nishimura's van, had a look into Leyte Gulf. He fired torpedoes at a radar ghost and concluded that there was nothing useful his two cruisers and four destroyers can do, so he retired down the strait. At 0433 the Americans, led by Oldendorf in his flagship, the cruiser *Louisville,* pursued the remnants of the Japanese Southern Force.

At 0330 Rear Admiral Tommy Sprague, in response to the order from Kinkaid sent at 0155, ordered Rear Admiral Felix Stump of Taffy 2, the center group, to conduct air searches to the north. An hour later, at 0430, Stump received Sprague's order, decides that *Ommaney Bay* is best prepared to do it, and sent her an order at 0509.

---

[40]Coleman, "Halsey at Leyte Gulf," 81.

Meanwhile Kinkaid, at 0412, in informing Halsey of the victory at Surigao Strait, asked if TF 34 is guarding San Bernardino Strait. Coincidentally, at that very time Mitscher ordered all TF 38 carriers to arm their first deck-loads for strikes at earliest dawn.

Ziggy Sprague's Taffy 3, the northern-most group of escort carriers, launched a combat air patrol for the ships in Leyte Gulf at 0530, and at 0545 Tommy Sprague moved all of the Taffys shoreward from their night positions, while Taffy 1, the southern-most group, launched a strike at the fleeing ships of the Southern Force. By 0607 Taffy 3 had launched planes for Gulf A/S patrol, as well as its own CAP and A/S patrols.

The Japanese were not idle. The Center Force spent the early morning hours steaming down the coast of Samar at 20 knots, and at 0644, just after dawn, began to deploy from columnar cruising formation to circular anti-aircraft formation. Moments later a lookout on the *Yamato* spotted the masts of Taffy 3. Before the change of formation could be accomplished, Kurita ordered "General Attack," and the Japanese lost formation and co-ordination as their ships charged down on the jeep carriers.

At 0645 lookouts in Taffy 3 were puzzled by anti-aircraft fire to the north; at 0646 *Fanshaw Bay* made an "unidentified surface contact" on her radar and her radio watch reported "Japs gabbing" on the fighter-interception net; and at 0647 an A/S patrol from *Kadashan Bay* reported the Japanese 20 miles north of Taffy 3.

At 0648 Halsey was puzzled to receive Kinkaid's message of 0412 asking whether TF 34 is guarding San Bernardino Strait.

Taffy 3 changed course to due east to open the range and launch aircraft at 0657, while at 0658 *Ommaney Bay* of Taffy 2 launched the ordered searches to the north (half an hour after sunrise) and Japanese battleships opened fire on Taffy 3. Ziggy Sprague broadcast an urgent contact report in plain language at 0701, and at 0702 Tommy Sprague, the Taffy commander, asked for and receives permission from Admiral Kinkaid to launch all available aircraft at Kurita's Center Force.

At 0705 Halsey sent a message responding to Kinkaid's inquiry saying that TF 34 is with him on the way north to attack Ozawa's carriers.

At 0707 Kinkaid sent a plain language message to Halsey that Taffy 3 was under fire from Japanese battleships and cruisers.

Up north, TF 38 scouts sighted Ozawa's Northern Force at 0710. Strike aircraft, already orbiting well ahead of the Task Force, were vectored in.

In the center, from 0715-0925 Ziggy Sprague 's Taffy 3, with air support from the other Taffys, fought a desperate action off the coast of Samar. His six escort carriers, three destroyers and four destroyer escorts fought off Kurita's four battleships, six heavy cruisers, two light cruisers and eleven destroyers through a combination of skill, heroics, and luck. After launching aircraft, Sprague turned south and then southwest, making smoke, dodging into rain squalls, and chasing shell splashes. The three escorting destroyers (and one destroyer escort) sallied forth to make torpedo attacks, shoot up the enemy, make smoke, and generally create chaos. Destroyer *Heerman* made a torpedo attack which caused the Japanese flagship, *Yamato*, to turn away from the battle for ten minutes, leaving Kurita seven miles behind the action and unable to coordinate his ships.[41] By the time Kurita got back on scene, the battle had become a melee. He decided to get the battle in hand, and at 0911 ordered "Rendezvous, my course north, speed 20." He milled about, dodging air attacks, until 1236 when the Center Force headed north back to San Bernardino Strait, attacked by air all the way and into the next day.

While Ziggy Sprague was fighting for this life, the messages from Seventh Fleet became ever more frantic as the morning wears on. Kinkaid sent a message to Halsey at 0725 saying Oldendorf's battleships were low on armor-piercing ammunition. And at 0727 Kinkaid radioed to Halsey in plain English: "Require Lee proceed top speed to cover Leyte; request immediate strikes by fast carriers." (This was before he could have received Halsey's response to his message of 0412.) Ziggy Sprague

---

[41]Thomas, *Sea of Thunder*, 286

radioed Halsey at 0735 that he is under attack by battleships and cruisers. And at 0739 Kinkaid radioed Halsey: "Help needed from heavy ships immediately." All of these messages go to Manus to be put on the Fox Schedule for Third Fleet.

TF 38's first strike swept aside a feeble CAP of 12 to 15 planes and bore in on Ozawa's Northern Force at 0800, sinking a light carrier and a destroyer, and damaging the heavy carrier and another light carrier.

At 0822 Halsey was shocked to receive Kinkaid's plain language dispatch of 0707 telling him Taffy 3 is under fire.

Kinkaid radioed to Halsey at 0829: "Situation critical, battleships and carrier strike wanted to prevent enemy penetrating Leyte Gulf."

TF 38 launched a second strike at 0835, and at 0848 Halsey ordered McCain's TG 38.1 to assist Seventh Fleet. (McCain was fueling hundreds of miles to the eastward and was unable to get his carriers to a launch position until 1030, and then another 90 minutes were required for the planes to reach their target.)

Kinkaid ordered Oldendorf to proceed with his Gunfire Support Group to a point a few miles north of Hibuson Island, at southern entrance to Leyte Gulf, and stand by at 0850, almost two hours after the Japanese attack Taffy 3.

Halsey received Kinkaid's 0727 plain language request for Lee's battleships and an air strike at 0900, and twenty-two minutes later he was alarmed to receive Kinkaid's message of 0725 concerning Oldendorf's lack of armor-piercing ammunition.

Halsey sent a message to Kinkaid at 0927 saying that TF 38 was engaged with Ozawa's carrier force more than 400 miles from Leyte Gulf, but that he had ordered McCain to assist Seventh Fleet.

At 0945 TF 38's second strike hit Ozawa's Northern Force. It crippled a light carrier and damages a light cruiser.

Kinkaid ordered Oldendorf to take about half his Task Group north to assist the Taffys at 0953, half an hour after Kurita had broken off the battle but before he definitely turned north.

At 1000 Halsey received Kinkaid's message of 0829, "My situation is critical." Halsey also received a message from Admiral Nimitz at Pearl inquiring as to the whereabouts of TF 34. This is the famous message in which the padding following the message, "the world wonders," was mistakenly left in by the decoder, causing Halsey to think that Nimitz had publicly rebuked him and leading to a scene of rage and tears on the flag bridge.

After getting himself back under control and thinking about it, Halsey ordered Bogan's TG 38.2, together with all six of Lee's battleships, to reverse course and steam south to help Kinkaid at 1055. (But even making best speed they would arrive too late to do any good.)

Bogan and Lee extracted their ships and head south to assist Kinkaid at 1115, but had to slow down to 12 knots to refuel destroyers at 1345. Meanwhile, between 1145 and 1200 TF 38 launched a third strike at the 14 ships of the Northern Force still afloat (including the heavy carrier and a light carrier). The third strike arrived at 1310, sinking the heavy carrier. A fourth strike was launched at 1315 and reached the remnants of the Northern Force at 1455, sinking the remaining light carrier and damaging one of the converted battleships. At 1610 TF 38 launched the fifth strike, which reached the Northern Force at 1710, causing some damage to one of the converted battleships but failing to sink anything. Davidson's Group 4 launched the last, small, attack, and although they clam a few hits they do little damage.

Lee completed refueling at 1622, and formed TG 34.5, which included *Iowa, New Jersey,* three light cruisers and eight destroyers under Rear Admiral Badger. They headed for San Bernardino Strait at high speed, covered by Bogan's carriers.

26 October

TG 34.5 arrived off San Bernardino Strait at 0100 (Kurita had already passed through the strait at 2140 the previous day), encountered the Japanese destroyer *Nowaki,* and sank her by gunfire at 0110. Badger's group turned south, but the other ships of Center Force had already escaped.

Aircraft pursued the fleeing remnants of the Japanese fleet, but the battle was over. And it had been a tremendous victory. Tactically, not only did the Americans hold their ground and complete the landings, but they sank one large and three light Japanese aircraft carriers, three battleships, ten cruisers and nine destroyers at a cost of only three carriers (one light, two escort), two destroyers, and one destroyer escort.[42] Strategically, with the loss of the Philippines the Japanese were cut off from desperately need oil and other natural resources of the Dutch East Indies. Admiral Toyoda, commander of the Combined Fleet, explained the Japanese situation and why they were willing to sacrifice the fleet at Leyte Gulf.

> "Should we lose in the Philippines operations, even though the fleet should be left, the shipping lane to the south would be completely cut off so that the fleet, if it should come back to Japanese waters, could not obtain its fuel supply. If it should remain in southern waters, it could not receive supplies of ammunition and arms. There would be no sense in saving the fleet at the expense of the loss of the Philippines."[43]

It was the end of the Japanese fleet,[44] which was no longer capable of influencing the course of the war. But still the question

---

[42]Thomas, *Sea of Thunder*, 322.

[43]Admiral Toyoda, in "Interrogation of Japanese Officials," Interrogation Nav No. 75, USSBS No. 378, p. 316.
   http://www.ibiblio.org/hyperwar/AAF/USSBS/IJO/IJO-75.html

[44]Morison, *Leyte*, 159.

remains: Why was Taffy 3 left to face the guns of Kurita's battleships and cruisers?

Decisions Made

We can see from the above narrative that there were actually a number of decisions taken by various people, within the context of a divided command, cumbersome communications between fleets, and Halsey's orders, the cumulative result of which put Taffy 3 under the guns of the Center Force. But it is necessary to examine certain key points in the narrative in more detail so as to understand the flow of events.

The planes of Halsey's TF 38 had pounded Kurita's Center Force in the Sibuyan Sea all through the morning and afternoon of October 24. By 1500 Kurita was retiring back up the strait. At 1512 Halsey's operations officer, Captain Ralph "Rollo" Wilson, sent out a "Battle Plan" to TF 38 and put it on the Fox Schedule for Admirals King and Nimitz.[45] The message read:

```
BATTLE PLAN. BATDIV 7 MIAMI, VIN-
CENNES, BILOXI, DESRON 52 LESS STE-
VEN POTTER, FROM TG 38.2 AND WASH-
INGTON, ALABAMA, WICHITA, NEW ORLE-
ANS, DESDIV 100, PATTERSON, BAGLEY
FROM TG 38.4 WILL BE FORMED AS TASK
FORCE 34 UNDER VICE ADMIRAL LEE,
COMMANDER BATTLE LINE. TF 34 TO EN-
```

---

[45]Potter, *Bull Halsey*, 239.

GAGE DECISIVELY AT LONG RANGES. CTG
38.4 CONDUCT CARRIERS OF TG 38.2
AND TG 38.4 CLEAR OF SURFACE
FIGHTING. INSTRUCTIONS FOR TG 38.3
AND TG 38.1 LATER. HALSEY, OTC IN
NEW JERSEY.[46]

Battleship Division 7 comprised the *Iowa* and *New Jersey*. So the plan was that four battleships, two heavy cruisers, three light cruisers, and fourteen destroyers be formed to fight the Japanese as they exit San Bernardino Strait. But the message didn't make clear when this would happen.

Although not an information addressee, because the plan did not affect his operations, Kinkaid's radioman decodes the message and shows it to Kinkaid.[47] Here the first unfortunate decision was made. Kinkaid, although the message is clearly labeled a "plan" and not an operations or battle order, assumed that the words "will be formed" were present imperative and not future indicative. He thought TF 34 has been formed and that his northern flank was secure against the Japanese Center Force, as did Nimitz and King. Others interpreted the message correctly. Vice Admiral Wilkinson, for example, formerly Halsey's com-

---

[46]Milan Vego, *The Battle for Leyte, 1944: Allied and Japanese Plans, Preparations, and Execution*, (Annapolis, MD: Naval Institute Press, 2006), 260, although Vego omits *Alabama* by mistake.

[47]Morison, *Leyte*, 290-91; Potter, *Bull Halsey*, 293; Cutler, *Battle of Leyte Gulf*, 160; Thomas, *Sea of Thunder*, 363-64.

mander of the Third Amphibious Force but now serving as Kinkaid's commander of the Southern attack group, understood the order correctly, but did not talk to Kinkaid about it.

There must also have been some doubt among members of Halsey's staff or among his task group commanders, for two hours later, at 1710, Halsey sent a clarification of his previous order by TBS to TG 38.2 and TG 38.4, the only two task groups affected by the plan and both close enough to be contacted by short-range radio: "If the enemy sorties TF 34 will be formed when directed by me." But since it goes out by TBS, neither Kinkaid nor Nimitz nor King receive it.

Meanwhile, Admiral Matsuda's two converted battleships and light forces from Ozawa's Northern Force were sighted at 1540, and the Northern Force carriers were found an hour later at 1640. At 1830 Halsey received flash reports on damage to the Center Force on the day's strikes: three battleships badly damaged and a light cruiser sunk.[48] This would seem to account for the fact the Kurita turned back from the strait. Although he started out with five battleships and ten heavy cruisers, due to submarine and air attacks he had three battleships badly beat up and only six heavy cruisers left.

So, the Center Force was badly damaged and retreating (Kurita actually turned back toward the strait at 1714, but Halsey

---

[48]Thomas, *Sea of Thunder*, 222.

wouldn't learn of that until the next morning) and the carriers had been found. What to do?

Halsey had three options.[49] The first was to use his whole force to guard San Bernardino Strait. He could have formed TF 34 to guard the strait, stationed one carrier group to provide air support against land-based aircraft and stationed the other two further out to fend off Ozawa's Northern Force carriers. This would have been in accordance with doctrine which emphasized concentration of forces and coordinated attack,[50] but it sacrificed mobility. And it could have simply been futile. Rollo Wilson, Halsey's operations officer, argued against this option, saying it would be like watching "a rat hole, waiting for the rats to come out."[51]

And meanwhile, what would Ozawa's carriers have been doing? With the American carriers were tied down, the initiative would have passed to the Japanese. Perhaps Ozawa would have sought a position where his planes, which without armor or self-sealing gas tanks were lighter and thus had a longer range than their American counterparts, could attack the American carriers without exposing his to counterattack. Or maybe he would just

---

[49]William F. Halsey, "The Battle of Leyte Gulf." U.S. Naval Institute Proceedings, May 1952,190. http://www.usni.org/magazines/proceedings/1952-05/battle-leyte-gulf; Thomas, *Sea of Thunder*, 218-21.

[50]Trent Hone, "U.S. Navy Surface Battle Doctrine and Victory in the Pacific," *Naval War College Review*, Winter 2009, Vol. 62, No. 1, 93.

[51]Thomas, *Sea of Thunder*, 218.

have done an end-run to the south and made a try for the shipping in Leyte Gulf himself.[52] If Ozawa had his full complement of aircraft, he ought to have had about 159 planes on deck.[53] (He had only 116 when he arrived,[54] but flew off a 76-plane strike at Sherman's TG 38.3, which flew on to Luzon to land.[55] So he had fewer than 30 planes on board when Halsey's carriers caught up to him. But Halsey wouldn't have known this until his attack the next morning.)

And besides, Halsey's orders clearly stated that if an "opportunity for destruction of major portion of the enemy fleet offers or can be created, such destruction becomes the primary task." In every major battle in the Pacific carriers had been decisive and in carrier battles it was vital to get in the first strike.[56] Waiting for the "rats," while it allowed concentration of forces, forfeited mobility and did not fulfill Halsey's orders. (We should also note that as these four carriers were among those that Spruance had let go at the Battle of the Philippine Sea, had Halsey let them go at Leyte, we'd still be talking about "Halsey's Decision.")

---

[52]Solberg, *Decision and Dissent,* 149.

[53]Willmott, *Battle of Leyte Gulf,* 73.

[54]Morison, *Leyte,* 191.

[55]Ibid. 192.

[56]Solberg, *Decision and Dissent,* 117. A lesson learned in inter-war fleet problems. See Albert A. Nofi, *To Train the Fleet for War: The U.S. Navy Fleet Problems* (Newport, RI: Naval War College Press, 2010) 125, 135.

The second option was for Halsey to divide his forces, leaving TF 34 and perhaps Bogan's TG 38.2 (at that time the smallest of the groups, as the Essex-class carrier *Bunker Hill* had been sent to Ulithi with exhausted aircrews,[57] and his two battleships and three light cruisers had been incorporated into TF 34) to cover San Bernardino Strait and take the other two groups north to strike Ozawa. Dividing naval forces went contrary to doctrine,[58] but perhaps was warranted in these circumstances.

However plausible at first sight, the idea of dividing Halsey's forces looks dubious on two grounds. First, McCain's TG 38.1 had not joined up, and with Bogan's group detached, Halsey was going into action with four large carriers and four light carriers and fewer than 500 planes.[59] This was a more than two-to-one advantage in aircraft (if Ozawa had his normal compliment of aircraft), but victory was not a forgone conclusion, and the case of the *Princeton* had recently shown that a single bomb can take out a carrier. Additionally, detaching TF 34 significantly reduced the anti-aircraft guns available to Halsey's carrier groups. By this stage in the war the fast battleships were recognized as essential anti-aircraft gun platforms for the fast carrier task groups.[60] In detaching TF 34, Halsey was giving up 43% of his 5"/38 barrels,

---

[57]Thomas, *Sea of Thunder*, 219.

[58]Halsey, "Battle of Leyte Gulf," 494-95.

[59]Coleman, "Halsey at Leyte Gulf," Appendix B, 113.

[60] Hone, "Surface Battle Doctrine," 74.

one of his primary anti-aircraft weapons.[61] This wouldn't have been prudent thing to do when seeking battle with Japanese carriers.

Halsey's third option was to use his whole force to destroy the Japanese carriers, leaving San Bernardino Strait unguarded. This option preserved concentration of forces and mobility, and fulfilled his orders to bring about "the destruction of major portions of the enemy fleet," but was a calculated risk. Halsey had the force to not only sink Ozawa's carriers, but to sink most of this other ships as well. But what would Kurita do?

The last Halsey heard, Kurita had turned back from San Bernardino Strait, but would he reverse course again? If he did, what would be the consequence? Halsey's staff, who had been reading Kinkaid's radio transmissions, knew that the Southern force of two old battleships and handful of supporting ships, was going to be greeted by Jesse Oldendorf's gunfire support group of six old battleships and numerous supporting ships shortly after midnight on 25 October. Even with Oldendorf's ships limited by the shortage of armor-piercing ammunition, it was reasonable to expect them to prevail. And even if Kurita reversed course soon, he couldn't have reached Leyte Gulf before about 1100 on 25 October.[62] That would have left him exposed to the

---

[61] See the Appendix for the make-up of the three task groups involved and TF 34's percentage of 5"/38 barrels.

[62] Thomas, *Sea of Thunder*, 221.

attack of the more than 400 planes of the Taffy's sixteen escort carriers (more aircraft than any one of Halsey's task groups)[63] for about five hours was and leave plenty of time to move Oldendorf's battleships into a blocking position. Halsey's staff was confident Kinkaid had the force to deal with Kurita.[64]

Additionally, Halsey's orders from Nimitz made it clear that the destruction "of major portion of the enemy fleet" was "the primary task." Ozawa's carriers were clearly that "major portion." The carriers were the most dangerous elements of the Japanese fleet, while the battleships had played little part in the battles of the Pacific.

Halsey made his decision. Just before 2000 he strode into the crowded flag plot, stabbed the chart with a blunt finger at the last reported position of the Northern Force, and said to Rear Admiral Carney, his chief of staff, "Here's where we're going. Mick, start them north." He then retired to bed, having had little or no sleep in the past 48 hours and expecting to rise shortly after midnight to prepare for the coming day's battle.[65]

All that remained was for Halsey's staff to draft orders and send them to his task groups, and to put a message for King, Nimitz and Kinkaid on the Fox Schedule telling them the situa-

---

[63].Wilmott, *Battle of Leyte Gulf*, 276. See also Morison, *Leyte*, 244 and 420-21.
[64]Thomas, *Sea of Thunder*, 220-21.
[65]Potter, *Bull Halsey*, 296; Thomas, *Sea of Thunder*, 226; Solberg, *Decision and Dissent*, 118-19.

tion and what was being done. Carney sent the following message at 2022: "Enemy force Sibuyan sea 1925 position 12 45N 122 40E course 120 speed 12 knots. Strike reports indicate enemy heavily damaged. Am proceeding north with three groups to attack enemy carrier force at dawn."[66]

Kinkaid received this message about 2105[67] and, because of his misinterpretation of Halsey's "Battle Plan" message of 1512, also misinterpreted the current message. What the writer had tried to convey was that the Japanese were headed back to San Bernardino Strait and that all of TF 38, all three carrier groups, was now headed north; the clear, but unstated, implication being that San Bernardino Strait was now unguarded. But Kinkaid had read Halsey's "Battle Plan" message as an order to form TF 34. In that light, Kinkaid, believing Halsey now has four groups, read Halsey's current message to mean that Halsey was proceeding north with the three carrier groups, and assumes that he had left TF 34, the battle line, to guard the strait.[68]

The 2022 order to concentrate the carrier groups and head north caused some consternation among Halsey's staff and subordinate commanders. Captain Mike Cheek, Halsey's intelligence officer, had just seen a report from *Independence's* night-flying scouts that Kurita's Center Force had turned back toward

[66]Solberg, *Decision and Dissent.* 119; Potter, *Bull Halsey*, 296.
[67]Vego, *The Battle for Leyte Gulf*, 268.
[68]Potter, *Bull Halsey*, 296.

the strait. He took this information to Halsey's air operations officer, Captain Doug Moulton and insisted that it be passed on to Halsey. A furious argument ensued in which Moulton refused to wake Halsey, saying that orders had already gone out and that anyway, the Center Force was finished and couldn't do any damage.[69]

Lieutenant Harris Cox, Cheek's deputy intelligence office, also thought the order was a mistake.[70] He had been studying a Japanese document, "Z Operation Orders," captured during the Battle of the Philippine Sea. The document clearly stated that the "primary objective" of the Japanese surface forces was to sink the invasion fleet at the beach while the carriers hovered over the horizon in support. He feared this was just the situation at Leyte Gulf and that Halsey was giving the Japanese a chance to execute their plan.

After talking the situation over with his roommate, Lieutenant Carl Solberg, Cox decided to go to Captain Cheek for one last try to persuade him to go up the chain of command. At about 2200 Cox and Solberg urged Cheek to appeal to Halsey's chief of staff, Mick Carney. Cheek did so, but either Carney refused to wake Halsey, or Cheek was given permission to wake Halsey but declined to do so.[71]

---

[69]Solberg, *Decision and Dissent,* 124-25; Thomas, *Sea of Thunder,* 390.
[70]Solberg, *Decision and Dissent,* 120-25.
[71]Ibid. 125; Thomas, *Sea of Thunder,* 229-31.

Shortly after the orders went out two of the Task Group commanders contacted the flagship. Admiral Bogan of Group 2 talked on the TBS with Captain E.C. Ewen of the *Independence,* whose night fliers were in his Group. Ewen confirmed his scout's contact report, and added the further ominous detail that the navigation lights in the San Bernardino Strait, long blacked-out, were now brightly lit. Bogan drew up a recommendation that TF 34 be detached with a couple of carriers to watch the Strait. He called the flagship over the TBS and personally read his message. A "rather impatient voice," one of Halsey's staff, said, "Yes, yes, we have that information." Feeling the brush-off, Bogan did not pursue the matter.[72]

Admiral Willis Lee's acute mind, sifting the intelligence data, figured out that the Northern Force was a decoy and the Center Force's reversal of course was temporary. He made a visual signal to the flagship with his views and got a perfunctory "Roger," merely acknowledging receipt of the message. After darkness fell Lee sent Halsey a message by TBS with his view that Center Force was coming out. Again a "Roger."[73] Lee did not press the matter further and his messages don't appear to have reached Halsey.

When the order to go north reached Vice Admiral Mitscher's flagship his chief of staff, Commodore Arleigh Burke, tried to

[72]Morison, *Leyte*, 195; Thomas, *Sea of Thunder*, 233.
[73]Morison, *Leyte*, 195; Thomas, *Sea of Thunder*, 231-33.

clarify the position of Kurita's Center Force. A few minutes later Burke received a contact report from *Independence's* night fliers (presumably the sighting at 1935). And at 2305 Burke again got confirmation (presumably from the 2120 contact) that the Center Force was headed for San Bernardino Strait. He took this information to Admiral Mitscher, who was asleep. Mitscher, who was cut out of the command of his beloved fast carriers when Halsey assumed tactical command earlier in the day, asked "Does Admiral Halsey have that report?" When told that he did, Mitscher said, "If he wants my advice he'll ask for it," then he rolled over and went back to sleep.[74]

There is no evidence that Halsey received the *Independence's* sighting reports that Kurita had turned back toward the strait. In fact, he apparently expressed regret to Admiral Lee sometime later that he had not been awakened.[75] There were probably several reasons he wasn't awakened. Some senior members of Halsey's staff were convinced that the order to proceed north was correct and that it was a waste of time to reopen the matter; others clearly felt that even if Kurita turned back the Seventh Fleet could handle his depleted force; and there was a reluctance to reopen an issue after a decision had been made. And clearly, some of his staff were trying to protect Halsey. He had been awake almost continuously for 48 hours and was facing a battle the next

---

[74]Morison, *Leyte*, 196; Thomas, *Sea of Thunder*, 236.
[75]Thomas, *Sea of Thunder*, 226.

day. The 62-year-old admiral was in desperate need of sleep and his staff was trying to see that he got a least a few hours.[76]

But his staff's reluctance to wake him had unfortunate consequences. The *Independence's* sighting reports, new and important information, never got to Halsey. Consequently and inexplicably, they were not forwarded to Kinkaid. Perhaps Halsey's staff was right and Kinkaid could handle the Center Force, but to plan for that eventually he needed to know the Japanese were coming. They had ample time to warn Kinkaid that the Center Force was headed south but they failed to do so. Kinkaid was caught by surprise and Taffy 3 had to scramble for its life.

Lastly, in this sad chain of events, the combination of Kinkaid's assumption that his northern flank was covered and Halsey's staff's poorly worded messages and failure to pass on to Kinkaid the warning that Kurita was coming through San Bernardino Strait resulted in a certain casualness in Seventh Fleet searches.

Admiral Kinkaid ordered only two searches to his north during these trying days. At approximately 1700 on October 24, PBY-5 Catalina "Black Cats" took off from their tender for a night search. Only one of the planes could have found Kurita's Center Force, but that plane, flying north along the coast of Samar, transited San Bernardino Strait between 2000 and 2030, before the Center Force arrived, and so had no chance of spot-

---

[76]Ibid.

ting them. Morison also notes that this plane was flying only 500 yards offshore and so was clearly looking for barge traffic and not a sea-going fleet.[77]

Admiral Kinkaid ordered only one other search to the north. At 0155 on October 25 he ordered Rear Admiral Thomas Sprague, commanding the 16 escort carriers, to launch three daybreak searches, one of them to cover the sector north of the carriers. At 0330 Sprague ordered Rear Admiral Felix Stump of Taffy 2, the center group, to conduct the searches. Stump received the order an hour later and decided that *Ommaney Bay* was best prepared to do it, and sent her an order at 0509. Due to squalls and trouble repositioning aircraft on the flight deck, the search didn't get off until 0658, nearly two hours later, half an hour after sunrise and at the very minute the Japanese battleships opened fire with their 18-inch guns on the northern-most group, Taffy 3.

It took a little more than five hours for the search order to be executed. Nor can the delay be blamed on communications, since the orders were going out not on the Fox Schedule but on intra-fleet frequencies. Taffy 3 launched a combat air patrol for Leyte Gulf at 0530;[78] Taffy 1 launched a strike against the retiring remnants of the Japanese Southern Force at 0545.[79] The

---

[77]Morison, *Leyte*, 289-90.
[78]Ibid. 246.
[79]Ibid. 245.

search could well have gotten off an hour-and-a-half before it actually did, and that may have made all the difference. But the lack of urgency is palpable, and that lack of urgency no doubt stemmed from the assumption that Halsey was watching the strait.

Too late, that assumption was found to be false. After the triumph at Surigao Strait, Kinkaid asked his staff around 0400 if there was anything they had overlooked. Kinkaid's operations officer, Captain Richard Cruzen, said, "We've never asked Halsey directly if Task Force 34 is guarding San Bernardino Strait."[80] Kinkaid put a radio message on the Fox Schedule at 0412 informing Halsey of the victory at Surigao Strait and asking if TF 34 was guarding San Bernardino Strait. Halsey received the inquiry almost two-and-a-half hours later at 0648, just ten minutes before the Center Force opens up on Taffy 3, and responded at 0705, saying that TF 34 was with him on the way north to attack Ozawa's carriers. Kinkaid had discovered that his assumption was false long before he read Halsey's message.

Judgments

At 0925 October 25 Ziggy Sprague was preoccupied with maneuvering Taffy 3 to dodge Japanese torpedoes when a signalman near the bridge yelled, "Goddamit, boys, they're getting away!" It took several minutes and a series of reports from cir-

---

[80]Thomas, *Sea of Thunder*, 244.

cling planes to convince him the Japanese had broken off the attack.[81] The surface action at Samar was over. Kurita milled around, constantly under air attack, trying to get his force in hand and deciding whether to continue the battle. But at 1310 he definitely turned north and retired toward San Bernardino Strait, pursued by air strikes all the way. The Taffys would still have to face kamikaze attacks that morning but they had survived the onslaught of the battleships and cruisers. They not only stopped Kurita's move to attack shipping in the Gulf, they sank three cruisers and heavily damaged three others, at the cost of an escort carrier, two destroyers and a destroyer escort.

It would not be long before people began to try to understand why Taffy 3 wound up facing the might of the Center Force. It seemed a simple thing: The Center Force transited the San Bernardino Strait and sailed undetected toward Leyte Gulf for almost seven hours before bumping into Taffy 3 because the strait had been left unguarded. It seemed obvious, as was said of the Earl of Cardigan's morning canter in the charge of the Light Brigade at Balaclava in 1854: "Someone had blunder'd."

That someone, it was thought in many quarters, was Halsey. The morning of the battle Admiral King was pacing up and down his office in Washington damning Halsey for his failure to guard San Bernardino Strait.[82] General MacArthur gave Halsey a

---

[81]Ibid. 288.
[82]Thomas, *Sea of Thunder*, 325.

"verbal castigation" for his "failure to execute his mission of covering the Leyte operations." Then, in an act of glorious hypocrisy, sent a public telegram of fulsome congratulation and expressing his "complete confidence and inspiration when you go into action in our support."[83]

But it must be said that after the war, both King and MacArthur changed their positions. King made a study of the battle and "reluctantly concluded" that Kinkaid bore much of the responsibility for the plight of Taffy 3, as by his failure to conduct air searches he "had failed to take the reasonable precaution that would have discovered the approach of the Japanese Center Force."[84] MacArthur, if he can be believed, later wrote said that he "never ascribed the unfortunate incidents of this naval battle to faulty judgment on the part of any of the commanders involved." Instead, he placed the burden on the divided command structure, where "two key American commanders were independent of each other, one under me, and the other under Admiral Nimitz 5,000 miles away, both operating in the same waters and in the same battle."[85]

Historians were no less harsh. Many followed Samuel Eliot Morison, who in his volume on the battle in his *History of U.S. Naval Operations in World War II,* wrote that "now that two ma-

---

[83]Ibid.

[84]Morison, *Leyte*, 289.

[85]Douglas MacArthur, *Reminiscences* (New York: McGraw-Hill, 1964), 230.

jor enemy forces were approaching from the north of Leyte Gulf, Halsey ignored the stronger and let it get between him and the Seventh Fleet, because he mistakenly assumed that it was the weaker, and 'no serious menace,'" and he suggests that "Halsey had enough gun and air power to handle both Japanese forces."[86]

But this sets the bar rather high. It is true that Halsey underestimated the strength of the Center Force. But all he had to go on were the flash reports from the airstrikes and the fact that Kurita was observed to turn back, which, Halsey had learned as commander of the South Pacific during the Solomons battles, was something the Japanese did not lightly do. It is also true that Halsey overestimated the strength of the Northern Force. But he could not have known that the four carriers had only 116 planes between them and that they flew off a 76-plane strike which went on to land on Luzon. The weakness of the Northern Force was only discovered on the morning of October 25 when Mitscher's attacking planes brushed a pathetically weak CAP out of the sky and found only two planes on the Japanese carriers' decks.[87]

As to his suggestion that Halsey had enough gun and air power to handle both Japanese forces, Morison seems as casual about TF 34 stopping the Center Force as Halsey's staff was about Kinkaid stopping the Center Force. A night battle at the

---

[86]Morison, *Leyte,* 193-94.
[87]Stolberg, *Decision and Dissent,* 163.

mouth of the San Bernardino Strait would not have been the massacre Surigao Strait was. The two forces were too evenly matched for that (four battleships, two heavy cruisers, three light cruisers and fourteen destroyers against four battleships, six heavy cruisers, two light cruisers and eleven destroyers). And Admiral Lee, who fought a night battleship engagement at Guadalcanal,[88] declined to do so at the Battle of the Philippine Sea because his force, made up of ships from four different task groups, had never trained together for a night engagement.[89] He was in essentially the same position at Leyte. And although he would have begun the battle with a tactical advantage, Lee cannot have been sanguine at the prospect, nor were some members of Halsey's staff.[90]

Morison comes closer to the truth when he says, "In conclusion, the reason why Kurita was able to sortie from San Bernardino Strait and steam toward Leyte Gulf for about seven hours, completely undetected, was a series of faulty assumptions on the part of his enemies."[91]

---

[88]Morison, *History of United States Naval Operations in World War II,* vol. 5, *The Struggle for Guadalcanal August 1942–February 1943,* (1958: repr. Edison, NJ: Castle Books, 2001), 270-285.

[89]Morison, *New Guinea,* 244; Hone, "Surface Battle Doctrine," 85.

[90]Carney, Halsey's chief of staff, opined that the numbers were "not good enough." Solberg, *Decision and Dissent,* 82.

[91]Morison, *Leyte,* 293.

Kinkaid assumed Halsey would "cover and protect" his landing forces by plugging the San Bernardino Strait, he assumed Halsey had done so by forming TF 34, and he further assumed that when Halsey said he was "proceeding north with three groups" to attack the Japanese carriers that he meant he was taking the three carrier groups with him but leaving TF 34 behind. And so certain was he in his assumptions that he made only the most feeble efforts to search to his north. Halsey was hardly better informed, assuming Kinkaid knew the Japanese were headed for the strait, that he had left the strait to pursue the Japanese carriers, and that Kinkaid could handle Kurita on his own.

But why all this assuming? In battle commanders have to make decisions based on faulty or incomplete information, or simply on educated guesses, as to what the enemy is doing. But to be forced to make assumptions about what your own forces are doing suggests that something is fundamentally wrong.

This flawed state of affairs as we have seen, stemmed from several sources. First, a divided command precluded an on-scene commander who could have seen to it that Halsey either guarded the strait or, if sinking the Japanese carriers was judged a more important objective, that Seventh Fleet be properly appraised of the situation in time to take the necessary defensive action. If politics and personalities prevented a united command, it was absolutely vital that the two fleet commanders communicate in a timely fashion in order to coordinate their forces. This was prevented by MacArthur's insistence that communication between the fleet commanders use the Fox Schedule rather than a dedicated frequency. But when "Where is TF 34?"—"On the way north with me" is a three-hour conversation, coordination in battle is going to be difficult.

Yet, even a divided command and cumbersome communications might not have led to Taffy 3 being exposed to battleship guns if Halsey hadn't been given conflicting orders. Had he been given orders only to "cover and protect" the landings and to "destroy enemy naval and air forces" threatening the landings, he might have construed his duties differently—or at least he would have been in clear violation of his orders had he left the strait unguarded to chase after Ozawa's carriers. But his additional orders making "destruction of major portions of the enemy fleet" his "primary task,"[92] combined with the divided command and clumsy communications, constituted a recipe for tragedy. And Nimitz's failure to require Halsey to coordinate his actions with Seventh Fleet, or at least inform Kinkaid of his actions, practically ensured a failure to coordinate the fleets.

The final element which led to this near-tragedy was some extremely weak staff work. Two pivotal messages, the "Battle Plan" and the message informing Kinkaid that Halsey was going

---

[92]Halsey clearly viewed his task as offensive. Halsey, "Battle for Leyte Gulf," 487.

north "with three groups," were poorly drawn and misunder-stood by some of their recipients.

It seems clear that Halsey's decision to go after the Northern Force carriers was not in itself wrong: it conformed to accepted naval doctrine of the day and fulfilled Halsey's explicit orders from Nimitz. But in the context in which it was made, the impli-cations of which no senior commander seemed to grasp, it re-sulted in unnecessary danger to the landings and the exposure of weak covering forces to an overwhelming enemy force. That Taffy 3 was left to face the big guns of the Center Force was more an organizational failure, a military misfortune,[93] than a simple blunder by a commander in battle.

After the battle Halsey ran into Ziggy Sprague on Ulithi while the fleet was in for rest and replenishment. Halsey approached Sprague and said, "Ziggy, I didn't know whether you would speak to me or not." "Why Admiral Bill, I'm not mad at you," Sprague replied. Halsey then said, "I want you to know I think you wrote the most glorious page in American naval history."[94]

---

[93]Eliot Cohen and John Gooch, *Military Misfortunes: The Anatomy of Failure in War* (New York: Free Press, 1990).

[94]John F. Wukovits, *Devotion to Duty: A Biography of Admiral Clifton A.F. Sprague* (Annapolis, MD: Naval Institute Press, 1995) 206.

And it is a glorious page. But it is a page that it was by no means necessary to write.

Appendix

TF 34 5"/38 barrels as a percent of available 5"/38 barrels at the time Halsey sends his "Battle Plan" message of 1512 24 October. Ships in bold are to be assigned to TF 34.

TG 38.2		TG 38.3		TG 38.4	
CV *Intrepid*	12	CV *Essex*	12	CV *Franklin*	12
		CV *Lexington*	12	CV *Enterprise*	12
CVL *Cabot*	0	CVL *Langley*	0	CVL *San Jacinto*	0
CVL *Independence*	0			CVL *Belleau Wood*	0
BB *Iowa*	20	BB *South Dakota*	20	**BB *Washington***	20
BB *New Jersey*	20	BB *Massachusetts*	20	**BB *Alabama***	20
CL *Vincennes*	12	CL *Santa Fe*	12	**CA *New Orleans***	8
CL *Miami*	12	CL *Mobile*	12	**CA *Wichita***	8
CL *Biloxi*	12	CL *Reno*	12		
Desron 52		Desron 50		Desron 6	
DD *Owen*	5	DD CL*arence E. Bronson*	5	DD *Muary*	4
DD *Miller*	5	DD *Cotten*	5	DD *Gridley*	4
DD *The Sullivans*	5	DD *Dortch*	5	DD *Helm*	4
DD *Tingley*	5	DD *Healy*	5	DD *McCall*	4
Desdiv 104		Desron 55		Desdiv 12	
DD *Hickox*	5	DD *Porterfield*	5	DD *Mugford*	4
DD *Hunt*	5	DD *Callaghan*	5	**DD *Bagley***	4
DD *Lewis Hancock*	5	DD *Cassin Young*	5	**DD *Patterson***	4
DD *Marshall*	5	DD *Preston*	5	DD *Ralph Talbot*	4
Desron 53		Desdiv 110		Desdiv 24	
DD *Halsey Powell*	5	DD *Laws*	5	DD *Wilkes*	4
DD *Cushing*	5	DD *Longshaw*	5	DD *Nicholson*	4
DD *Colahan*	5			DD *Swanson*	4
DD *Uhlmann*	5				
Desdiv 106				Desdiv 100	
DD *Stockham*	5			**DD *Caperton***	5
DD *Weiderburn*	5			**DD *Cogswell***	5
DD *Twining*	5			**DD *Ingersoll***	5
DD *Yarnall*	5			**DD *Knapp***	5

TG 38.2		TG 38.3		TG 38.4	
5"/38 barrels	168	5"/38 barrels	150	5"/38 barrels	144

Available 5"/38 barrels   **462**
TF34 5"/38 barrels   **200**
TF34 percent of available barrels   **43.2%**

Bibliography

Interrogation of Japanese Officials, Interrogation Nav No. 75, USSBS
  No. 378, p. 316.
  http://www.ibiblio.org/hyperwar/AAF/USSBS/IJO/IJO-
  75.html

Investigation of the Pearl Harbor Attack. Report of the Joint Committee on the Investigation of the Pearl Harbor Attack, 79th
  Congress, 2d Session. S. Doc. 244, vol. 3.
  http://www.ibiblio.org/pha/pha/congress/part_0.html.

Bates, Richard W. "The Battle for Leyte Gulf October 1944. Strategical and Tactical Analysis." Unpublished Research Document,
  U.S. Naval War College, Newport, RI: 1953. vol. 1.
  http://www.ibiblio.org/hyperwar/USN/rep/Leyte/NWC-1.pdf.

Cohen, Eliot and John Gooch. *Military Misfortunes: The Anatomy
  of Failure in War.* New York: Free Press, 1990.

Coleman, Kent Stephen. "Halsey at Leyte Gulf: Command Decision and Disunity of Effort." Master's thesis, Fort Leavenworth,
  KS, 2006. http://www.dtic.mil/cgi-
  bin/GetTRDoc?Location=U2&doc=GetTRDoc.pdf&AD=ADA
  463797

Cutler, Thomas J. *The Battle of Leyte Gulf: 23-26 October 1944.* Annapolis, MD: Naval Institute Press, 1994.

Halsey, William F. "The Battle of Leyte Gulf." U.S. Naval Institute *Proceedings*, May 1952. http://www.usni.org/magazines/proceedings/1952-05/battle-leyte-gulf

Hone, Trent. "U.S. Navy Surface Battle Doctrine and Victory in the Pacific." *Naval War College Review*, Winter 2009, Vol. 62, No. 1.

Hornfischer, James D. *The Last Stand of the Tin Can Sailors*. New York: Bantam Books, 2004.

MacArthur, Douglas A. *Reminiscences*. New York: McGraw-Hill, 1964.

Morison, Samuel Eliot. *History of United States Naval Operations in World War II*, vol. 4, *Coral Sea, Midway and Submarine Actions May 1942–August 1942*. 1949: reprint, Edison, NJ: Castle Books, 2001.

———. *History of United States Naval Operations in World War II*, vol. 5, *The Struggle for Guadalcanal, August 1942--February 1943*. 1958: reprint, Edison, N.J.: Castle Books, 2001.

———. *History of United States Naval Operations in World War II*, vol. 8, *New Guinea and the Marianas, March 1944–August 1944*. 1958: reprint, Edison, N.J.: Castle Books, 2001.

———. *History of United States Naval Operations in World War II*, vol. 12, *Leyte, June 1944–January 1945*. 1958: Reprint, Edison, N.J: Castle Books, 2001.

Nofi, Albert A. *To Train the Fleet for War: The U.S. Navy Fleet Problems*. Newport, RI: Naval War College Press, 2010.

Potter, E.B. *Bull Halsey: A Biography*. Annapolis, MD: Naval Institute Press, 1985.

Robertson, D.C. "Operations Analysis: The Battle for Leyte Gulf." Unpublished Research Document, U.S. Naval War College, Newport, R.I.: 1993.
http://www.ibiblio.org/hyperwar/USN/rep/Leyte/OpAnal.pdf

Solberg, Carl. *Decision and Dissent: With Halsey at Leyte Gulf*. Annapolis, MD: Naval Institute Press, 1995.

Thomas, Evan. *Sea of Thunder: Four Commanders and the Last Great Naval Campaign 1941–1945*. New York: Simon & Schuster, 2007.

Vego, Milan. *The Battle for Leyte, 1944: Allied and Japanese Plans, Preparations, and Execution*. Annapolis, MD: Naval Institute Press, 2006.

Willmott, H.P. *The Battle of Leyte Gulf: The Last Fleet Action*. Bloomington, IN: Indiana University Press, 2005.

Wukovits, John F. *Devotion to Duty: A Biography of Admiral Clifton A.F. Sprague*. Annapolis, MD: Naval Institute Press, 1995.

www.ingramcontent.com/pod-product-compliance
Lightning Source LLC
Chambersburg PA
CBHW060040050426

42448CB00012B/3089